BE NOT AFRAID

Mary Martina Dockter

ISBN 979-8-99072-977-3 (paperback)
ISBN 979-8-99072-978-0 (eBook)

Copyright © 2024 by Mary Martina Dockter

All rights reserved. No part of this publication may be reproduced, distributed, or transmitted in any form or by any means, including photocopying, recording, or other electronic or mechanical methods without the prior written permission of the publisher.

DEDICATED TO OUR BABY SISTER
JOANNA MARIE
WHO DIED SOON AFTER HER BIRTH

Contents

BE NOT AFRAID 1
ABBA 2
FATHER 3
NAZARENE 4
MESSIAH 5
DO NOT FEAR 6
LIGHT IN THE DARKNESS 7
BEYOND 8
ROAD TO HEAVEN 9
LAND OF THE LIVING 10
ONE WAY 11
THE HIGH WAY 12
ROAD TO PERDITION 13
THE LONG RUN 14
IN THE LONG RUN 15
FEAR NOT 16
HOME IS WITHIN 17
SEARCH WITHIN 18
IN THE NAME OF 19
LUCKY ONE 20
AIM HIGH 21
I BELIEVE 22
CHILD LIKE 23
YOUNG AT HEART 24
LIFE IS A HOOT 25
THE BEST DAY 26
AN EAR FULL 27
THEY COME 28
THE GUARDIANS 29
VOICE OF SILENCE 30
INFINITE INTELLIGENCE 31
THE RING OF SOLOMON 32

EYES OF GOD	33
GOD'S STARE	34
THE ELYSIAN FIELDS	35
E.T. PHONE ROME	36
WE ARE NOT ALONE	37
THE SENTINEL	38
RECKONING	39
POWER TO COMMAND	40
GET BEHIND ME	41
GENUFLECTION REFLECTION	42
SHALL BLOOM	43
HUMAN WALL	45
UNITY	46
HELPING HANDS	48
THE LORD'S DAY	49
COMMUNION	50
HOLY HOST	51
THE HAND OF GOD	52
FINGERPRINTS	53
THE HAND DEALT	54
HOLD MY HAND	55
OPEN ARMS	56
GOD'S NEAR	57
LUMINESCE	58
WELCOME	59
HEAVENLY	60
LUMINESCENT	61
GOD'S GIFT	62
JOYFULNESS	63
HIS GIFT	64
DOUBLE OR DIRE	65
LIVING YEARS	66
SOUL FRAME	67
CANVAS CLOUDS	68
THE AIR SHARES	69
LIVING BREATHING	70

WITHIN WITHOUT	71
PRECIOUS BLOOD	72
THE TRUTH	73
LIFE	74
FOREVER YOUNG	75
MY LIFE	76
THE TREE OF LIFE	77
GENESIS' END	78
FORBIDDEN FRUIT	79
FAMILY TRAGEDY	80
JUSTICE	81
CAIN'S STAIN	82
THERE'S NO THERE, THERE	83
BORN AGAIN	84
NEWS FLASH	85
GOOD NEWS	86
AS ABOVE SO BELOW	87
A PERENNIAL ECOLOGICAL MARVEL	88
LIFE'S GARDEN	89
HARMONY	90
I AM PERFECTION	91
THE CROWN OF ADVENT	92
CHILD OF TIME	94
ELYSIUM'S CHRISTMAS	95
ALTRUISTIC	96
BE THE ROCK	97
FOLLOW ME	98
FISHER OF MEN	99
DISCIPLE	100
REVEALING JUDAS	101
REVEALING CAIAPHAS	102
REVEALING PONTIUS PILATE	103
HOLY FACE	104
WHIT	105
THE LANCE	106
COME FULL CIRCLE	107

MOTHER MAY I	108
THE NEW EVE	109
MORNING STAR	110
PORTRAIT OF MARY	111
THE SUDARIUM	115
THE SHROUD OF TURIN	116
TRANSFORMATION	117
REIGN DOWN	119
SEA OF GALILEE	120
LOCH NESS GUESS	121
APOCRYPHAL	122
BOOK OF ENOCH	123
SAVE ME	124
DIMENSIONAL DARKNESS	125
BE ON GUARD	126
BLESSED BE	127
END TIMES	128
APOCALYPTIC	129
LESSNESS	132
PURIFICATION	133
SO BE IT	134
INEVITABLE	135
SHEOL	136
SHILOH	137
UTOPIA	138
UNVEILING	139
TO DIE IS TO LIVE	140
HERE AFTER	141
TIMELESS	142
EVER AFTER	143
ETERNITY	144
INFINITE	145
MOMENTOUS	146
PASSING BY	147
PASSING AWAY	148
DEAD END	149

STAY AWAKE	150
DEATH CAN DANCE	151
QUIESCENCE	152
EVANESCE	153
HEAVEN'S WAY	154
WHERE DO WE GO	155
HEAVEN'S MYSTERY	156
NOTHING FOR GRANTED	157
LET THINGS BE	158
DEAD SPACE	159
DEATH WILL COME	160
REVENANT	161
BRING ME TO LIFE	162
ONE'S SAFETY BOX	163
CLOSURE	164
RIDDANCE	165
DECLUTTER	166
PEACEFULNESS	167
HEARTFELT	168
DIVINE DIRECTION	169
PEACE OF MIND	170
A FATHER'S LOVE	171
BEHIND HER, HE STOOD	172
LOVE	173
PLUMS AND ROSES	174
MOTHER	175
LOVE ME MOMMY	176
A MOTHER'S PRAYER	177
LITTLE PRAYER BOOK	178
MORNING	179
BY MY SIDE	180
FORGIVE ME	181
OUR GUARDIAN ANGEL	182
LIVING MEMORY	183
JOANNA	184
WITH WINGS TO GO HOME	185

ANGEL EYES	186
SEQUENT	187
DANCING IN HEAVEN	188
JUST LIKE	189
FAMILIES ARE FOREVER	190
REMEMBER SEPTEMBER	191
FORGIVENESS	192
FAMILY REUNION	193
LIFE WILL BE	194
SOMEWHERE	195
NO WHERE	196
WHAT MAY BE	197
HEAVENLY HEIGHTS	198
ANGEL OF CHAOS	199
THE FINAL COUNTDOWN	200
WHAT MATTERS MOST	201
HOLY OF HOLIES	202
WHAT MATTERS	203
LOVE MATTERS MOST	204
THE DEAD	205
NEARLY TIME	206
A QUESTION	207
DEAD TIRED	208
MY LAST BREATH	209
MY DEMISE	210
WEAR RED INSTEAD	211
AFTERLIFE	212
PROCUL HARUN	213
REMEMBER ME	214
LIFE AND DEATH	215
VIA DOLOROSA	216
PRECIOUS WOUNDS	217
THE GOOD BOOK	218
LEVITICAL	219
BASIC INSTRUCTIONS BEFORE LEAVING EARTH	220
REST IN PEACE	221

HOME FREE	222
VICTORY AND DEFEAT	223
NEVER ALONE	224
ANGEL FEATHERS	225
GIFT OF COINS	226
SALTY ADVICE	227
PHARAOH	228
THE ESSENES	229
UNDAUNTED	230
EXODUS	231
CRUCIFIED SUICIDE	232
ABBA vs. ALLAH	233
THE SCREAMING ABDABS	234
TAKE ME HOME	235
LOOK UP	236
FREE AT LAST	237
TEARS OF JOY	238
COMING HOME	239
CERTITUDE	240
NO LONGER AFRAID	241
SAFE AND SOUND	242
DIMENSIONAL	243
HOME FOR THE HOLIDAYS	244
WELCOME HOME	245
NO REASON TO BE AFRAID	246

BE NOT AFRAID

This world may be a scary place to be.
When, a sea of worry is drowning me.
No one is there to give a helping hand.
And it's even worse being on the land.

But, there is hope, if one does believe.
We follow in footsteps, He does leave.
And He calms a sea of worry we wade.
In a scary world we live, be not afraid.

2023

ABBA

Abba is our Father the creator of everything.

From the beginning of time His existence is to bring.

His cosmic energy is transforming a universe.

For He lit up the darkness with stars we will observe.

And His creation of planets gave forth a birth.

A home for humanity with all its beauty we call earth.

2024

FATHER

There is but one Father from up above.
He is our true Father that we're to love.
As He loves us for we're His, His alone.

We are a children of God we are known.
To be like our Father we must then obey.
The commandments He gave and to pray.

2024

NAZARENE

To be a follower of Christ, one must take up their cross.
And be not afraid of what may follow them or their loss.
For one's reward in the end is greater than here on earth.
As their soul will be made new so death will be a rebirth.
When Jesus died on the cross and His resurrection began.
It's beginning to those who follow His teaching the plan.

2024

MESSIAH

He has come, to be the savior of mankind.
And born in the lowliest of places we find.
He is the son of God but not to be the king.
For He's here on earth as a servant to bring.
Children of the world free from hell's pain.
We are forgiven of our sins, heaven to gain.
By His love for us as the sacrifice He made.
The way, truth and life a promise God gave.

2024

DO NOT FEAR

There's no reason for anxiety to succumb.
When, the One who's risen He has begun.
To change the lives of the many who hear.
Follow Me as I preach to you, do not fear.

For the world will try to sweep you away.
Its current of corruption with lies to sway.
You're on the wrong path for hate is near.
But if you'll follow Him, then do not fear.

2023

LIGHT IN THE DARKNESS

Do not be afraid, when you are alone.
For you're never alone as it is known.
When someone is close that is so near.
By one's heart there is nothing to fear.

In the dark, but darkness, will be gone.
Like the stars in the sky before a dawn.
Do not be afraid, when alone the night.
When within one's heart will be a light.

2023

BEYOND

Look ahead instead of glancing over the shoulder.
Its past road has been traveled this trek now over.
Stake claim with a wish upon the million of stars.
Keep an eye upon the prize no doubt one goes far.
So be not afraid what one's fears may bring upon.
Go ahead and take a new path and travel beyond.

2009

ROAD TO HEAVEN

From the time we are born, we are on a trip.
And pray we're on the right path, equipped.
For the voyage is a straight and narrow path.
As there are many ways to stumble in wrath.

That'll try and steer you away from the goal.
And enter into the pearly gate by one's stroll.
On the road to heaven, is where ecstasy to be.
The final destination, when our life is set free.

2024

LAND OF THE LIVING

There is no dying when one dies.
For, one's demise is life realized.
We enter into a place no grieving.
After death is a land of the living.

2024

ONE WAY

There is but one way to leave this place.
It's without breath within death to face.
The world beyond it's where we will go.
But no one knows, heaven or hell shows.

Just like death the way to heaven is here.
Or the road to hell is here, also with fear.
So one must take the high road each day.
And travel straight narrow path one way.

2024

THE HIGH WAY

On the road thru life there are many paths.
Where, one is safe and the other a bypath.
You can take one, for the fun, of a joyride.
Where, chances of an accident, will abide.
Or do you take a slower way and be good.
Where it might be less traveled but would.
Be safer in the long run when on the road.
Where, life has many paths along its way.
Know there's a wrong way or the high way.

2023

ROAD TO PERDITION

From the time we are born, we are on a trip.
And pray we're on the right path, equipped.
But sometimes we take the wrong way path.
For the voyage is much easier even its wrath.

That has steered us away from a pearly gate.
When, straight and narrow is much, too late.
On the road to perdition is where death to be.
The final destination when hell has deceived.

2024

THE LONG RUN

Life is a race and the finish line is death.
In a marathon that will end out of breath.
It doesn't matter if the road taken up hill.
Or path that's level eventually it will still.
Lead all to the same place where it's done.
As your living life racing for the long run.

2023

IN THE LONG RUN

Generally speaking, there is nothing to fear.
When, thinking of the future perfectly clear.
Life as we know it will end and be renewed.
In death will be a catalyst on this journey to.

A world without worry and pain we do feel.
For heaven there's joy in the love that heals.
When, thinking of the future, perfectly clear.
Generally speaking, we have nothing to fear.

2023

FEAR NOT

What is there to fear, but fear, itself?
It's only power unknown of yourself.
Once you say its name and take it on.
It runs to find a victim to take along.

For, it cannot control one in control.
When, you face fear a different role.
So be in charge, the key to yourself.
What is there to fear, but fear, itself?

2023

HOME IS WITHIN

Home is within
For there you begin
To know one self
The love for yourself
A place in the heart
Forever never part
For there one begins
Home is within

2011

SEARCH WITHIN

No need, to go outside of your realm.
When, deep inside you may find them.
It is there you will feel strength to fly.
And live out your dreams if only to try.

For therein oneself is the key to unlock.
The very essence others do try to block.
So take courage to discover your perch.
By looking within instead as you search.

2023

IN THE NAME OF

All that we see, touch, taste and hear,
Comes from above and makes us real.
Everything on Earth is created by Him,
By His bread of life is where we begin.

Look around, the many gifts we share,
But without Him, none would be there.
So be thankful and so grateful because,
All that we have here is in the name of.

2023

LUCKY ONE

There once was a man who had riches galore
But did little to enrich his life, or others more
He spent his time within the walls of its stone
Worried his estate taken, he never would roam
And died alone with all the money in the world
Forsaken and forgotten lying in a casket burled

There once was a man who had no riches at all
But that didn't stop to enrich him or others call
He spent his time helping those without a home
Worried their peace of mind taken it was known
And died the richest man for all that he has done
Never forgotten or forsaken, he is, the lucky one

2023

AIM HIGH

Aim for heaven,
And all things on earth are possible!

2020

I BELIEVE

I BELIEVE
A new day begins, the morning sun rises.
The gift of life wins when our spirit arises.
And we breathe essence of all that is great.
With so many presents when we're awake.

I BELIEVE
The glistening dew kisses a radiant flower.
As honey bees flew pollinating by the hour.
For the petals decorate land with every hue.
A blanket of color began, timeless and new.

I BELIEVE
All God's creatures walk, and fly on earth.
They have so many features different births.
It's an imagination beyond, wildest dreams.
This world we belong, this wondrous thing.

I BELIEVE
Mankind is to rule taking care of this place.
But we are here to be a tool, to be His face.
A new day begins as the morning sun rises.
I do believe in Him my grateful heart arises.

2019

CHILD LIKE

To enter into the gates of heaven
Not a penny is needed for one to be
Able to walk through a pearly vision
And greeted by Jesus, so lovingly

One may think it is a person wise
Maybe a teacher or a preacher good
But one does not come to realize
The heart is the key that would

Unlock its gate to enter God's home
And hear angels sing in paradise
Held in the arms of Jesus it's known
To be in heaven one must be child like

2024

YOUNG AT HEART

Days go by faster than one can count.
Before you know it, time's in amount.
Larger than one wishes the number be.
Wasn't it yesterday you were just tiny.
And playing games and joking around.
Being free, living life a way it's bound.
Its freedom of youth not meant to part.
If one lives their life, be young at heart.

2021

LIFE IS A HOOT

Live life like a bird,
For life's a glorious word,
And let your worries go free,
Whatever they may be,
Live a simple life,
Less stress less strife,
So smile and sing to suit,
Life is a hoot!

2012

THE BEST DAY

The sun shines on my face
All my troubles are erased
With a blue sky I do eye
A butterfly and bird fly by
There's a skip to my walk
A cheerful smile as I talk
For life is happy and clever
When, it's the best day ever

2012

AN EAR FULL

Dreams are angels,
Whispering in your ears,
Never stop listening,
Always keep believing!

2020

THEY COME

From heaven to earth they come.
As angelic beings to protect has begun.
When, we kneel to pray in the night.
They are a light in the dark from fright.
For a song we hear are with wings.
As they flutter in sync, while they sing.

2024

THE GUARDIANS

They are there even though they are unseen.
Is their desire not to be noticed it does seem.
As caretakers they help guide and protect us.

In a world that is on the verge to destroy us.
We are not alone, they are among to defend.
And save the multitude angels are guardians.

2024

VOICE OF SILENCE

Within oneself is a silent voice
For, right or wrong is a choice
Which do you choose if asked
From angel or devil the tasked
And walk along a straight road
Or crawl by the evil one's load

2023

INFINITE INTELLIGENCE

Thank God for God for I weep to think naught.
I'd fear if we were alone within this vast vault.
But maybe, just maybe what is happening here.
Will be for our own good its lesson made clear.

We to think it is man the one who is in control.
Like a child among elders who has a lesser role.
We're part of a plan but without our intelligence.
For, it is God in control the one with infiniteness.

2009

THE RING OF SOLOMON

At birth one is anointed with a ring.
It is a gift from God to all that sings.
The ring of Jupiter is deep and clear.
And found on the index finger here.

      High Intelligence
      Literary and Art

If the ring is in a semi circle found.
Your emotions on your face bound.
You take to heart all that is so near.
And live a life on your sleeve dear.

      Talented Showmen
      Pursuit in Music

But if the ring is light and unnoticed.
You may not be given gifts with this.
The foresight within is not very keen.
For you're not like the others deemed.

      Intelligence and
      Mysticism not Strong

If by chance, you have a double ring.
This reveals you're sixth sense brings.
You can always turn bad luck to good.
No matter how many of failures stood.

      Astrologist, Numerologist
      And Psychologist

      2019

EYES OF GOD

The eyes of God look down upon man.
He has been there since the beginning began.

2023

GOD'S STARE

The crash of thunder can be heard a hollow roar above the earth.
A deity awakes from His slumber to unfasten heaven's gate girth.
The innocent souls below swallowed by a creature's jaw of steel.
Aware of their demise when it comes to mankind's wicked deals.
But many will not be forsaken taken from the brimstone of Hades.
As the dead come to life their spirits will be with Him not in Haiti.
For then the crash of His thunder will roar as He hears our prayers.
When the gate of heaven is reopened and we are under God's stare.

2010

THE ELYSIAN FIELDS

Do you sometimes look up into the sky and wonder?
Is there a place beyond this one here way up yonder?
Is this as good as it gets, this world we live on earth?
Is the life we have now, the only one since our birth?
Is death an end of our existence blowing in the wind?
Is dying a door to enter heaven a new life will begin?
Is there a place beyond this one here way up yonder?
Do you sometimes look up into the sky and wonder?

2023

E.T. PHONE ROME

Ring, ring! Ring, ring! Is anybody out there?
Within the universe of outer space somewhere.
For this time the church will pick up your call.
They decided extraterrestrials are real after all.

2018

WE ARE NOT ALONE

Have you ever wondered, if we're the only ones?
Who inhabit this universe from the time it begun?
We came upon this one planet from all of the rest.
I wonder who'd decide this one would be the best.

Have you ever wondered, if we are apart of a plan?
Who would inhabit this planet to be known as man?
We came to become keepers, of lesser ones known.
I wonder are we, but the same, for we are not alone.

2023

THE SENTINEL

Humanity is not alone in this vast conceived dome
Eyes gazed stones upon souls composed of bones
Mankind is held in hand hence granules of sand
For mortal destiny has a plan dealt to each man
To be blown in the wind so breath of life can begin
Existence begets its origin as vital flame within sin

As a supreme being gapes a celestial sphere creates
And all its seeing cannot relate to the verity of fate
Be our life force is full and unaware to who'll
In reality is the one to rule for free will is cruel
This seed of silence reversed amid a truth so adverse
We need only converse to the sentinel of the universe

2003

RECKONING

I reckon,
My life needs,
Checking!

2006

POWER TO COMMAND

You have the power to command the evil one.
To voices in your head, say do wrong is done.
It is within your self and find strength be free.
When, you cry out to Satan, "Get behind me."

2024

GET BEHIND ME

Living at large it has a price to pay
They deny they have lost their way
His claws are deep under your skin
For his plan to forsake you to begin
But realize there is hope with a plea
Tell him these words, get behind me

Living for Christ has a reward, pray
He will not be denied this He'll say
His love for us is stronger than a sin
For His death gave new life to begin
And realize there is hope with a plea
He spoke these words get behind me

2023

GENUFLECTION REFLECTION

I kneel for God alone for mankind souls are stone.
So no one's greater than others sisters and brothers.
We must share this soiled place as one human race.
Or soon it won't be long, if we all don't get along.
We'll end up killing each other one after the other.
Because, one believes color of skin mankind's sin.
Will, give them the right to abolish black or white.

2020

SHALL BLOOM

Born in the ghetto of the universe,
her body felt the fire of hatred
and the coldness of loneliness.
She roams through the darkness with
no hope of blooming.
Tears rain from her eyes,
flowing rivers and ducts of oceans.
Her skin quivers
at the thought of never being
touched by hands, deprived of
becoming a world.
Pounding footsteps by God,
pierce her heart. Blood oozes from her
pores as His feet seep into
her longing flesh.
She cannot let him go.
He is the destroyer of darkness,
her hope of blooming.
Scooping tears in her hand,
she offers Him drink, for He has
traveled many miles and is
weary of thirst.
Trickles of water sprinkle
down His chin as He watches
her every move.
As though He has read her mind,
the cup is thrown from His hands.
They embrace and become
One.
She has been fertilized and the
gift of the sun warms the seed.
God has planted and she
Shall Bloom a garden.

2

The day came when the seed inside
her grew to a plant with many
flowers. The pains of labor roared
thunder as her children emerged
from her womb, burying themselves
into her flesh. She names them
Man.
Her children were not identical.
Those who display their color
with supremacy made ridicule
of their brothers, birth marked
from her labor. They have
been born in the ghetto of
their mother's flesh, feeling the
fire of hatred and the coldness
of loneliness. They roam through
the darkness with no hope of blooming.
Tears become rain, splattering death
as it drowns life. Their skin quivers
at the thought of never being touched
with justice, deprived of becoming equal.
Pounding footsteps in protest
pierce their brothers' heart. Blood
oozes from their brothers' pores
as hands grip into their flesh.
They cannot let go. They must
tear away the darkness and
find the dream of blooming.

1973

HUMAN WALL

Each man is a fence, tainted with his greed.
Wired, stoned, wooded in the seed.
Inherited by blood to all.
Mayhem is painted upon the human wall.
The paint is prejudice.
Its torch was to burn into my no longer flesh.
No God spewed fury bellowing from the hills.
I was not to die on this cross. I am their will.
My body nailed to bodies on each side.
Their motives no longer can hide.
I was to be baptized.
Paint was brushed into my eyes.
The distemper burned as it gave me light.
Man in duress captured my sight.
Paint was brushed into my ears.
The distemper burned as I began to hear.
I was to hear prejudice my first word.
Taught exactly the way the sound should.
Paint was brushed onto my tongue.
The distemper burned as animosity begun.
I saw myself begin to shout.
Taunting and jeering with, flout.
Paint was brushed onto my hands.
The distemper burned as fetter demands.
I saw myself repressing man.
I have done what they command.
Within throe, prejudice weighed me off the cross.
I felt the nails become loose and lost.
I fell from the fog and gloom.
Born from my mother's womb.
Not wired, stoned, wooded, I am flesh.
I will not hold my brother's hand in prejudice.
A blemish upon the human wall.
Never mended, each fence will demise and fall.

1975

UNITY

Earth is a building of gray mist
Mankind is of three pigeons
White for knowledge
Black for joy
Yellow for peace
The pigeon of white builds his nest
On the North window
Knowledge is the key
To the door of this building
Thought the white pigeon
The pigeon of black builds his nest
On the South window
Joy is the key
To the door of this building
Thought the black pigeon
The pigeon of yellow builds his nest
On the East window
Peace is the key
To the door of this building
Thought the yellow pigeon
And the three pigeons of mankind
Separately tried their keys
But the locked door fore
West would not open

2

Bricks of gray mist
The air of prejudice
Their polluted eyes could not see
The building of Earth was cold from the mist
So the three pigeons of mankind began
To fly to the chimney
For the warmth from inside
Their wings like fingers touched in flight
And the knowledge of the white pigeon
The joy of the black pigeon
And the peace of the yellow pigeon
Gave birth to one spirit
Unlocking the Elysian door
The keys from each pigeon united together
Become heaven's hearth of love
Heaven is the hearth inside
The building of gray mist
Mankind is to be one
White for knowledge
Black for joy
Yellow for peace
United together for love

1975

HELPING HANDS

There will always be the one to stand
Whatever the task whatever is asked
Whatever the work whatever it took
Whatever the pain whatever is slain
Whatever the cost whatever crossed
By your side and guide helping hands

2023

THE LORD'S DAY

On the seventh day God rested and reflected.
Of many bountiful gifts on earth He detected.
Oh it pleased Him so to witness what is done.
Our earthly home is where humanity's begun.

So that is the day we should set aside to pray.
Sometime, in our busy schedule, it is to obey.
Since, He Himself, put aside the time, to rest.
Shouldn't we, celebrate, The Lord's Day, best.

2024

COMMUNION

As was told in the First Epistle to the Corinthians,
The Last Supper, final meal in the Gospels begins.
When Jesus came to Jerusalem hailed as their king,
It was, at this table, His trial and tribulations bring.

For during the Passover, they came together to eat,
And during the meal Jesus predicts who will deceit.
But, before they begin, He will, wash the feet of all,
Judas who betrays him and Peter will deny His call.

The Three Synoptic Gospels is a Eucharist account,
Of when Jesus breaks bread and gives it in amount.
"Love one another as I have loved you," be renewed,
By saying to them, "This is my body, given to you."

Jesus shared with Disciples, before His crucifixion,
It is a scriptural basis for the Eucharist that's begun.
For it's the body and blood of our Lord Jesus Christ,
We partake, Holy Communion we're given new life.

2024

HOLY HOST

By the hand of God we are given bread.
"This is my body given to you." He said.
We are fed with the Holy Spirit renewed.

Our lives will never be forsaken but new.
It is within the Eucharist and Holy Ghost.
We are reborn in Jesus with the holy host.

2024

THE HAND OF GOD

He is there to take our hand when life is no longer in our command.
For the night takes over with its starkness leaving us in its darkness.
But by His promise the light will be, there to help and to set us free.
If only we let go of pride's fraud, and be saved, by the hand of God.

2023

FINGERPRINTS

The hand of God illuminates
the night.
As stars and planets and galaxies
come to be.
And creating this eternal vortex
of a universe.
Begins the earth with its moon
and everything.

The hand of God wipes away
tears of rain.
With every droplet accumulates
in the deep.
He fills the rivers and ocean with
liquid life.
In the beginning is the fingerprint
of everything.

The hand of God metamorphosis
the land.
Its enigma in this alien world is
our birth.
Organisms to dinosaurs to apes
then man.
A divine plan is the evolution
in everything.

The hand of God illuminates
the night.
As stars and planets and galaxies
come to be.
And creating this eternal vortex
of a universe.
Begins the earth with its moon
and everything.

2018

THE HAND DEALT

One should deal with the hand they are dealt.
For life is one, big gamble, it is how it is felt.
Do you look, on the bright side, or enter dark.
A place, where there is, no escape, to embark.
So play its game with thoughts one must deal.
With the hand they are dealt in a positive feel.

2024

HOLD MY HAND

We are never alone in this world of ours.
From the time we are young until the hour.
To go beyond and we start a new life.
And be without pain, be without strife.

God is there a parent holds a child's hand.
To help one cross the street or to help stand.
And will take our hand at the crossover.
When entering into death and life is over.

2023

OPEN ARMS

Dying so peaceful here in the dark
My life is now over and ready to embark
On a new journey but I won't be alone
So there won't be a reason to worry or moan
For the pathway is bright to show me the way
To a heavenly gate I pray that I may
Be greeted by Him and be so very warm
And told that I am home with open arms

2024

GOD'S NEAR

Every time I see blue skies above,
I see a blanket in clouds of His love.

Every time I see majestic mountains high,
I see a reminder He is always nearby.

Every time I see the green grass and trees,
I see a symbol to why we fall to our knees.

Every time I see the vast oceans of blue,
I see a vision of many blessings from you.

Every time I see the rippling rivers flow,
I see the abundant gifts we've come to know.

Every time I see a precious baby lie,
I see a sign of His power the reason why.

Every time I see family and friends dear,
I see His mirror image for God is near.

2019

LUMINESCE

A soul is bright light in all of us
A burning star within that glows
For mankind was born luminous
From each man's lifeblood flows

Our mother the earth we all love
Gave birth to her children a night
Our father is the universe above
God's plan in humanity is might

A soul is bright light in all of us
A burning star within that glows
For mankind was born luminous
From each man's lifeblood flows

2003

WELCOME

All are welcome in this place to be with Jesus to see His face.
But one should realize there is a price He forgave sins advice.
Sin no more when He told them go live your life and to show.
By His blessing you are renewed to sin no more was His clue.
To be with Him liken heaven on Earth and to be anew rebirth.
All are welcome in this place to be with Jesus, to see His face.

2024

HEAVENLY

I can only imagine how wonderful heaven will be.
Beyond any imagination as anyone could ever see.
I close my eyes and try to picture the beauty found.
But it is more majestic than anything that is around.
I close my eyes, and try to listen to His angels sing.
But it's more angelic than anything I hear can bring.
I close my eyes, and try to feel the love, that will be.
But it is more than anything on earth, it is heavenly.
I can only imagine, how wonderful, heaven, will be.
Beyond any imagination, as anyone, could ever see.

2024

LUMINESCENT

Like a baby's smile beaming sight.
Like a mother's eyes shares delight.

Like a butterfly's wings as in flight.
Like an eagle soaring as if it's light.

Like a forest growing by its height.
Like a mountain majestic by might.

Like the sun by day warmth invite.
Like the moon in darkness is white.

Like a star that shines in the night.
Like a comet's tail glowing bright.

2023

GOD'S GIFT

The most wondrous gift God gave to man.
It's not a gift one is able to hold in a hand.
Nor pick it up to rip open wrapping paper.
Even though, it is decorated, by His labor.

For, He has given us the waves of the seas.
And birds in the air that dance on a breeze.
And a forest green with its bounty of trees.
So I thank God for His gift, for all of these.

2021

JOYFULNESS

I sing and dance, to the music in my soul.
When joy's in my heart I'm out of control.
For, the song is a sparrow's sweet melody.
As I fly from a body without care and free.
Nothing in this world can destroy my nest.
My life is complete with God's joyfulness.

2024

HIS GIFT

His gift to you is this.
It's the day of your birth's bliss.

2023

DOUBLE OR DIRE

Be aware of one's given gift of abilities
Silver pieces bestowed at birth as stabilities
Compare oneself to one of the three servants
Burying one's soul or investing merchants
Which will it be when divinity asks to hire
Double one's gifts in life or live life in dire

2005

LIVING YEARS

It's within a lifetime that one has the chance.
To express in words, their love will enhance.
Each other's lives as they travel on this road.
Together by journey through life how it goes.

Don't leave behind feelings, you will, regret.
Take the time to tell your love ones here yet.
They may pass on, to the other side, you fear.
So let them know this love in the living years.

2024

SOUL FRAME

Listen to me people, all around the world.
Just get onboard and let love, be the word.
For, love is the essence, of all that is good.
Where there is love the heart is understood.
So take your neighbor's hand on this train.
And let your love shine, your soul's frame.

2023

CANVAS CLOUDS

One's soul is like a painter's dream.
For God is the painter, it does seem.
He takes His brush and dips in love.
He paints everyone as clouds above.

For, we are His canvas by our lives.
With each stroke His love is realized.
Our beauty within is His masterpiece.
As angelic clouds so then all may see.

2024

THE AIR SHARES

A gift to us all the minute we are born.
For, life takes its first breath before clothes are worn.

2022

LIVING BREATHING

This thing called life is quite a special gift.
That most of us take for granted.
We simply go thru the day without one lift.
Of a thought or a prayer ranted.

And thank the creator for the creation of life.
We are apart of this cosmic plan.
But we're just a smidge in its universal blithe.
So we must make each day grand.

By living and breathing with a joyful heart.
Knowing the end could be near.
For if we look back, not ahead, a new start.
Our lives will be living so clear.

This thing called life is quite a special gift.
That most of us take for granted.
We simply go thru the day without one lift.
Of a thought or a prayer ranted.

2022

WITHIN WITHOUT

Look within yourself to find what you need.
He is there, the one, whose blood, did bleed.
For without Him there is nothing from Earth.
That really do matter not even our own birth.
We are just a smidge, within a universal plan.
If we live, without Him, we are meager man.

2023

PRECIOUS BLOOD

Within the body a red river flows.
It carries life's energy we to grow.
We become steadfast like the tree.

And branch out, to be you and me.
For the veins within is like a flood.
That carries a most precious blood.

2023

THE TRUTH

Age is what you make it
Keeping a body and mind fit
Secrets of eternal living
Is not taking but giving
To yourself and others

Share life with all around
And more life will abound
Hold on to the truth
Not to lose your youth
By giving yourself to others

2002

LIFE

Living
Is
For
Everyone

2005

FOREVER YOUNG

Hold on to the truth
Not to lose your youth
A mind keeps you young
Being the silent tongue
The body has no age

As long as you believe
The mind can conceive
Forever young is the plan
Make it a habit on hand
Not to turn another page

2002

MY LIFE

Was it not I who was born at my birth
When, I took my first breath here on Earth
I became a person right from the start
This is a journey with the beat of my heart

No one can claim that they are also me
Even those born from the same family tree
For this is my gift from a creator above
It is my life and I choose to fly like a dove

2023

THE TREE OF LIFE

There is one tree on this planet, existence unknown.
But if it no longer exists our lives would be so alone.
And not even matter to another but is scattered about.
Our lives would be drifting nowhere dying, no doubt.
The tree of life is the gate keeper, of everyone's soul.
It is the spirit of our being, with each leaf that grows.

2022

GENESIS' END

The beginning, the Euphrates river flowed.
And on judgement day, there, war explodes.
A Place Adam and Eve eat the garden seeds.
A world's demise. A place, mankind bleeds.
And on judgement day, there, war explodes.
The beginning, the Euphrates river flowed.

2005

FORBIDDEN FRUIT

In the middle of a garden was a tree bearing fruit.
But it's forbidden to be eaten so it's not in pursuit.
When, there's plenty of other food within its gate.
So, Adam never became hungry, or Eve, his mate.

As the story goes they are faithful to the command.
Until, a visitor that is a snake slithers upon the land.
And temps, the woman in saying take a bite and see.
How wonderful to be like God taste and you will be.

Then it became clearer not only did she eat the seed.
For as the serpent tempted her, she enticed his need.
And when Adam gave into his desire and took a bite.
They no longer were in heaven, but hell was in sight.

2022

FAMILY TRAGEDY

Once, there was this man and wife.
A man and wife are barren by strife.

For many years they tried for a son.
As many years God's plan is undone.

So this man for himself takes a slave.
And a son is born from his misbehave.

But his wife is told she will bear a son.
This man's in disbelief for she is done.

When a child is born he has two sons.
So one must go God's plan has won.

Once, there was this man and wife.
And tragedy today is from their strife.

2007

JUSTICE I

Come with me brother, brother come with me.
I have something to show you, something to see.
You will be the first to die.
You will be with God and His lie.
His justice for all as He spits in my face.
But He smiles at you, there will be no trace.
I am jealous.
I am furious.

JUSTICE II

WHERE IS YOUR BROTHER?
I am not my brother's keeper.
Why don't you seek for yourself?
You are God.
The One who knows all things.
YOU WILL NOT DIE CAIN.
DEATH WILL NOT BRING PAIN.
THE LAND NO LONGER GROWS FOR YOU.
PEOPLE WILL CURSE YOU. I WILL PLACE A CLUE.
SO THEY MAY KNOW YOU AMONG US.
I AM JEALOUS.
I AM FURIOUS.

1975

CAIN'S STAIN

Your sin passed on from generation to generation.
A brother against a brother is man's abomination.
For this jealous rage within must make an amends.
If we are to live together, then peace should begin.
Forgive the past. It's not meant to last, a reminder.
We are here in this world, only, to help each other.

2007

THERE'S NO THERE, THERE

An empty vessel is a person without a soul.
One who is heartless and it's out of control.
By living their life as if, no one else is there.
Not thinking of its consequences to not care.
But we're here together no one is ever alone.
Even if one thinks they are, a truth is known.
A person's never empty when a soul's where.
There's always hope in redemption it's there.

2023

BORN AGAIN

The womb within the soul is our rebirth.
For it's there one will be reborn on earth.
A spiritual infant held in the arms of love.
We're children of God, from father above.
And our mother is the new Eve we begin.
To live a life with Him we are born again.

2024

NEWS FLASH

BEEP, BEEP
LIFE IS A TEST, IT IS ONLY A TEST
AND YOU WILL BE ADVISED FOR ANY EMERGENCY
THIS HAS BEEN UNIVERSAL BROADCAST MESSAGE
FROM GOD'S COMMUNICATION SYSTEM
BEEP, BEEP

2006

GOOD NEWS

Awake to hear what is in store.
To those who'll listen to what we're for.
We're children of God here on Earth.
It is our birthright since our birth.
And from that day forward with our breath.
We will live forever after our death.

2024

AS ABOVE SO BELOW

On earth is bound by the universal light.
That shines afar within the dark of night.
It was created by our God in seven days.
To be a home for humanity, it was made.
For it is there, our existence began anew.
As above so below, the planet's life grew.

2024

A PERENNIAL ECOLOGICAL MARVEL

How, wondrous is this planet of ours
This gift our home an amazing flower
It blooms in spring and in summer lie
With brilliant colors before winter die
But, it never fails to come back to life
When, dormant, this perennial is alive

2023

LIFE'S GARDEN

How wonderful to be living in this space.
The Earth is our home blest by God's grace.
For the seeds of our birth are planted within.
As fruit of His creation our lives to begin.

We are His bountiful harvest in the bloom.
Our souls shine from His love under the moon.
And we are nourished with gifts given to us in.
We're the beautiful flowers in life's garden.

2024

HARMONY

All in order, rest assured
Life will follow His direction
Do not worry, blest assured
Like the flower we are perfection

2010

I AM PERFECTION

I am perfection
I am this image

I am luminous
I am the universe

I am the night
I am the star

I am the sun
I am the day

I am the ocean
I am the river

I am the mount
I am the forest

I am the valley
I am the flower

I am the cloud
I am the earth

I am the universe
I am luminous

I am this image
I am perfection

2008

THE CROWN OF ADVENT

A wreath of candles, symbolize, the passage to Christmas Day.
The four Sundays of Advent, a Christian tradition is displayed.
It respectfully represents the coming of Jesus as a baby so mild.
And with each colored candle is lit, we remember Mary's child.

The first candle is of the color purple for violet is a liturgical hue.
It signifies a time of prayer, penance, and sacrifice, we should do.
As it is sometimes called the "Prophecy Candle", those it reflects.
When Isaiah foretold the birth of Christ the candle is of hope kept.

The second candle is also the color purple, and is lit to tell where.
It is called the "Bethlehem Candle" a reminder their travels there.
For Mary and Joseph went to Bethlehem, a journey, they did take.
That is why a second candle is lit, representing faith for their sake.

2

The third candle is the color pink for rose has a special place here.
For the third Sunday of Advent is to remind us we should not fear.
It is called the "Shepherds Candle" and meant for joy to everyone.
So rejoice, this "Gaudete Sunday" with the birth of Christ to come.

The fourth week of Advent we light the last purple candle we see.
To mark the final week is the "Angel Candle" we wait for it to be.
With The birth of our Savior and the message of angels will bring.
"Peace on Earth, good will toward men" His angels they will sing.

The white candle in the middle of the wreath is lit Christmas Eve.
As the candle is called the "Christ Candle" and represents lovingly.
The life of Christ for the color white is for purity His birth to begin.
For Jesus Christ is our Lord and King, our Savior pure without sin.

2023

CHILD OF TIME

Sweet child of time unaware of the world's crime
Asleep in a manger's stall will be savior for us all
Mankind is blind and crying but His angels flying
Will be multitude of believers to thee we'll be free
From a crown He wears shines sweet child of time

2023

ELYSIUM'S CHRISTMAS

I can only imagine how glorious it will be
To celebrate the holiest day in history
Among the twinkling stars that I see
With Jesus at His party

A chorus of seraphim we sing along
Chanting lyrics the Happy Birthday song
The days are bright and the night is gone
With Jesus we belong

Golden tables with celestial wings
White, puffy clouds to sit and sing
Overflowing with food and drink angels bring
With Jesus we want for nothing

For the greatest gift ever adored
Was wrapped in swaddling clothes worn
Christmas in Heaven blow the horn
With Jesus we are reborn

I can only imagine how glorious it will be
To celebrate the holiest day in history
Among the twinkling stars that I see
With Jesus at His party

2019

ALTRUISTIC

The one true, unselfish act, granted to mankind
Began as a child born in a manger until his time
To begin his ministry on Earth to save our souls
From fires of hell, and died on the cross to show
His love for us, beyond any love that is on Earth
That began when he was a child, granted at birth

2024

BE THE ROCK

Be the one who is strong.
Be the one hatred's gone.
Be the one carries a load.
Be the one a path showed.

Be the one beacon's light.
Be the one who does right.
Be the one they may mock.
Be the one the mighty rock.

2023

FOLLOW ME

Along the seashore they threw their nets.
These fishermen believed livelihoods set.
Until a man walked up to them, and said.
I will make you fisher of men, by his led.
And follow me, for I am the bread of life.
If you follow me into heaven no one dies.

2024

FISHER OF MEN

It began at the Jordan when Jesus appeared before John.
To be baptized by him so His mission on earth has begun.
And even though, John refused at first because of his sins.
He tells him, he must do this, for God's demands to begin.
For, Jesus is to cast a net into the water not to catch a fish.
But to be its teacher as His life's journey is heaven's wish.

As He treks along the Sea of Galilee He sees two brothers.
Simon and Andrew throw their net into the sea as it hovers.
And glides into the water, they are told, to follow this man.
They are fishermen but this man reveals He has a new plan.
Come after me and I will make you fisher of men, He cries.
He has chosen disciples to finish the mission, when He dies.

2022

DISCIPLINE

One must have inner discipline to be the chosen few.
To follow in His footsteps, a life no one really knew.
On a journey that will test the very essence of a soul.
Only in the afterlife is the promise of eternal control.
With the blessings of bliss granted to the chosen few.
They are disciples of discipline, God's spiritual crew.

2023

REVEALING JUDAS

A man is chosen among the twelve to be the traitor.
For the hour has come with raised fists against him.
The perfume not sold, its fragrance still lingers later.
A reminder to the silver pieces soon will be his win.

But, he stole from the purse with no regard the poor.
Therefore his selfish heart, not comprehend his state.
And why God chose the demise for this somber soul.
When his heart realized, it will be done, it is too late.

2010

REVEALING CAIAPHAS

A man is chosen among the Sanhedrin to be the traitor.
For, the hour has come so Pharisees not be against him.
The high priest plan is sold, its prophecy to linger later.
A reminder to the council, a heretic arrested is his win.

But, he denied all of the signs with no regard, the poor.
Therefore, his egotistic heart, not comprehend his state.
And why, God chose the demise, for this, pietistic soul.
When his heart realized what will be done, it is too late.

2010

REVEALING PONTIUS PILATE

A man is chosen among the Romans to be the traitor.
For the hour has come the public will be against him.
The custom to release a criminal sold, to linger later.
A reminder to the rabble, he, washed hands, his win.

But, he crucified the Savior, with no regard the poor.
Therefore a hardened heart, not comprehend his state.
And why God chose the demise this procurator's soul.
When his heart, realized, what was done, it is too late.

2010

HOLY FACE

She wipes the blood and sweat off His face.
As He, carries the cross to that dreary place.
On her veil an image imprinted on the cloth.
Revealing pain and suffering by one's swath.

The face of Jesus is not made by man's hand.
For it's a gift to mankind by God's command.
The Veil of Veronica reminds us of who bled.
He saved us from sin by rising from the dead.

2019

WHIT
(With Him in Time)

Splinters are we, fragments of the tree.
Our hands gather dust, suffer we must.
In order to gain, so in life there is pain.
All humans to bleed, we die by a creed.
But, death not lost because of the cross.
For lowly are we whittled from the tree.
A message is obeyed there is displayed.
In the end we fly splinters from His eye.

2009

THE LANCE

Do not break His legs, His mother begs.
He's without a breath, succumb to death.
He's died on the cross, for His life is lost.
As the crowd scatters, so will this matter.

If a lone soldier aims, a wound his shame.
How God would show, in mercy to know.
His forgiving of all sin, even when it's in.
He pierced with lance, His son by chance.

To be converted amen, a new life to begin.
He falls to his knees, in His blood he sees.
Heaven within earth, His death is his birth.
Then hope is for us, with our St. Longinus.

2020

COME FULL CIRCLE

The star of Bethlehem shines bright in the sky.
His Father above reigns in love from on high.
He looks down at His son just born in a stable.
As a babe wrapped in swaddling clothes, able.
He feels the warmth of a mother holding Him.
But, He is protected by a father from evil sins.
Mary lays Him in the wood so all man can see.
For, Joseph stands there by their side, silently.

The storm in Golgotha scatters, those, nearby.
His Father above reigns with wrath from high.
He looks down at His son just died on a cross.
As a son wrapped in swaddling clothes is lost.
He feels no warmth from mother, holding him.
But, we are, protected by His Father from sins.
Mary cradles Him in her arms, from the wood.
For, Joseph has given his tomb it's understood.

2020

MOTHER MAY I

When, I was a child I played many games.
And friends would join in the fun the same.
There was one game played, many a times.
We'd stand close together in a straight line.
But one would be in front of all of the rest.
To be like a mother, in questions we'd ask.
And if by chance our request were granted.
Like prayers we pray in what we so ranted.
I was a child playing and she heard my cry.
For, there's a mother above, Mother may I.

2024

THE NEW EVE

Mary, the mother of God is forever blest.
She wears a crown in heaven now to rest.
The matriarch, Eve, for she is, of the new.
She is the morning star that shines so true.

2024

MORNING STAR

Bright she illuminates, from up above
For her beauty shines with all her love
She looks down from high to us below
As a glorious star with a brilliant glow
The mother of Jesus, like morning dew
Our morning star, her son, makes anew

2023

PORTRAIT OF MARY

Her miraculous story begins within the town Nazareth of Galilee.
For God's messenger Gabriel is sent to the one who will believe.
Thereupon the sixth month time this angel did appear before her.
Enlightened above, announcing a blessed child, conceived to stir.
A daughter chose amid the sky to carry the ruler, over those wary.
The Holy Spirit came upon the virgin servant be known as Mary.

Although, betrothed to a man named Joseph, that hour was alone.
If she's conceived before they were married, she could be stoned.
His decision to grant divorce, is unwilling to expose her to the law.
Thus, being proclaimed, take her as your wife, in a dream he saw.
When he awoke from the vision, as a husband, begot any relations.
She was to give birth to a son, a prophecy fulfilled by a revelation.

2

During the age of Caesar Augustus, census is held in every town.
Twas Joseph the lineage of David, to Bethlehem they were bound.
Their arrival is greeted by the words, no room for them in the inn.
For her time bearing a child completed, and soon to be at its end.
She gave birth to her first born son, laid him in a manger to sleep.
While all heaven's angels rejoiced, the demons within man weep.

A mother cradles her son, wrapped in swathe clothes amid hay.
By many shepherds paid homage throughout the night and day.
Astrologers from the East arrive to present their gifts from afar.
In search of the newborn King, they had followed his rising star.
The reign King Herod proclaimed the massacre of younger boys.
Joseph and Mary flee to Egypt, a child saved for mankind's joy.

3

Every year, the couple would return to Jerusalem for the Passover.
A celebration shared with family, a crossing when the feast is over.
They begin their journey home, with faith a son is among relatives.
Unknown by parents, the child will be found where the Father lives.
His mother searches among the party. Her fears are tears of sorrow.
As tears become jovial, keeping all things in memory for tomorrow.

A mother is touched by the Spirit at a wedding in Cana of Galilee.
For a proud woman asks her son to give the command to believe.
The stone jars are empty and she explains to him there is no wine.
They are filled with water, a miracle witnessed, it is now his time.
He gives the sign, as choice wine is served last among the guests.
It is the beginning to his end, a mother's blight, by her son's test.

4

The guards arrest and bound her son, he's sent to the high priest.
She is there to witness their accusations and prays for his release.
An innocent man is brought before the stone pavement of Pilate.
A criminal charge beheld as King of the Jews, he did not deny it.
For within the crowd she fears the plea, her son the King to die.
His life is in their hands as a mother hears. He will be crucified.

Weaving a crown out of thorns, he's sent out to carry his cross.
Upon the site of The Skull Place, a mother weeps a son's loss.
As soldiers strip him of his clothes, they nail him to the wood.
An angry storm disperse the mob, a mother and new son stood.
A woman chose mid the sky to watch the ruler over those, wary.
The Holy Spirit upon his mother is forever the portrait of Mary.

2007

THE SUDARIUM

He is taken off the cross and held in the arms of His mother.
She holds Him for the last time as blood and tears intertwine.
His lifeless body is carried to the tomb for it'll be discovered.
A piece of linen cloth covers the head of Jesus will be divine.

It will not display an image unlike The Shroud of Turin does.
But it will contain male blood that matches a holy conundrum.
For is this the relic that covered the sacred face where He was.
Before, rising from the dead and leaving behind the Sudarium.

2020

THE SHROUD OF TURIN

Hidden within its thread

Lies a man alive or dead

Its history

A mystery

The cloth survived years

Stain with blood and tears

His crime

He's divine

Evidence is not allowed

To prove it is His shroud

2019

TRANSFORMATION

Ruthless and heartless he's the killer of believers.
He possesses evil power,
He's a religious terrorist with the plans to deliver.

It's violent persecution to Christians in Jerusalem.
He leads a revolt this hour,
Those liable of blasphemy are to be stoned by him.

When as a boy he held coats of the men who stoned.
Saint Stephen to his death,
So now he drags men and women from their homes.

To be sent to prison found guilty squashed on sight.
No longer souls by breath,
So by his actions these Christians will see his might.

But on the road to Damascus the risen Lord appears.
And he falls to the ground,
"Saul why do you work so hard against me," he hears.

As he answers, "Who are you?" "I am Jesus the one."
His voice he heard around,
You're hurting yourself trying to hurt me with some.

Then he said, "What, do you want me to do, Lord?"
He's told to get up this time,
And go into the city where orders will be his reward.

Saul got up from the ground and he opened his eyes.
And he was stricken blind,
They took him by hand and led him there as he cries.

He didn't see for three days and couldn't sip or eat.
But in a dream it is revealed,
That there was a man the Lord did want Saul to meet.

This man's in disbelief for Saul put many in chains.
He is the one, I have sealed,
To hear who are not Jews, Kings and Jews, my name.

2

So Ananias went to the house where Saul was led.
For the Lord had sent him,
By the Holy Spirit he sees again and once again fed.

It is then Saul begins to preach in the Jewish places.
Love Jesus repent your sins,
All who hears him were surprised with shocked faces.

This the man who beat and killed those he preached.
That Jesus is the son of God,
But Saul kept growing in power so this he did teach.

His edifying infuriates the Jews so they want to kill.
And make plans to then rob,
So they watched at the city gates to take his free will.

But followers helped him get away during the night.
In a basket over the wall,
And from then on he preached without fear the light.

For, he is a warrior for Jesus Christ the almighty Lord.
And his weapon his call,
As he, does battle with his words and not by the sword.

And from this Saul becomes homeless and persecuted.
When a friendship begins,
He finds kinship with St. Luke for both are cultivated.

Together they preached good news to the lost heathen.
In Jesus Christ without sin,
For St. Luke's devotion to this man, he did believe in.

Their common bond is a fellowship with the blest one.
A goal they live towards,
They may even die for because the battle must be won.

The road to Damascus gave to us the one called Saul.
By Jesus our Savior Lord,
It is from his holy transformation, known as St. Paul.

2020

REIGN DOWN

Droplets of His love fall upon the earth

Raindrops from heaven quench our thirst

A spirit is full with blessings from above

His reign we bow down to Oh gentle dove

2020

SEA OF GALILEE

Upon its banks lies the river Jordan.
Its water levels becoming, shortage.
Does, this mean an antichrist comes.
For, in the story of Jesus, it's begun.

This is where He walks on the water.
And He calms a storm by His barter.
He gives the disciples bountiful fish.
In the miracle He shows is His wish.

But the painting, Rembrandt, is lost.
The Storm on the Sea of Galilee cost.
To this day, it has never been found.
A devil laughs when it's not around.

But the Bible doesn't tell it that way.
By the Sea of Galilee it was His day.
And His miraculous mission on earth.
It began in stormy waters our rebirth.

2021

LOCH NESS GUESS

From ancient times of Scottish lore
A creature is told, from long before
The written word, on paper and pen
But it's depict, stone carved by men

The mysterious entity first is known
In an account by St Columba shown
For it did appear a biography written
By an account a swimmer was bitten

Another attack was soon to be made
St. Columba ordered a beast to obey
"Go back" he said, the monster fled
And because of this, the story's led

To many sighting of a Nessie today
It is a dragon, sea serpent some say
Or a plesiosaur dinosaur at its best
The Loch Ness monster just a guess

2022

APOCRYPHAL

There are stories in the Bible thought to contain.
As doubtful authenticity of creation, and is vain.
They are widely circulated, read across the land.
But are shunned, and not to be believed, by man.
Do not be afraid of the chapters that are blocked.
There is truth to behold, from the prophet Enoch.

2023

BOOK OF ENOCH

The origin of demons and giants he did tell.
And why some angels from heaven did fell.
The great-grandfather of Noah visions were.
Of the great flood that came to destroy occur.
In the fall of the Watchers angels fathered us.
We were Nephilim as "sons of God" on earth.
Before a deluge we were "daughters of men".
Within biblical times a story how man began.
And as Enoch visits heaven in a dream form.
His insight and revelations guide us and warn.

2020

SAVE ME

We are drowning, in a sea of corruption.
Right and wrong is blended to be as one.
There're no absolute truths to hold on to.
Whatever, one believes is gospel for you.

I'm bobbing for a third time calling help.
As I plead for someone to save me I yelp.
Then the waters become calm when I see.
He has been there all along watching me.

2024

DIMENSIONAL DARKNESS

From here to there, there's a maleficent world.
To a demonic pit is where lost souls are hurled.
And cast into a sea of fire, but there is no light.
Only one breathes sulfur from an endless night.

Of horrific torture, the screams of those bound.
They have chosen their fate no longer be found.
To a demonic pit is where lost souls are hurled.
From here to there, there is a maleficent world.

2023

BE ON GUARD

Stay alert when not knowing the hour.
For, this day or the night might be our.
Last time here on Earth and be judged.

By every sin to those we have grudged.
A time for one's sleep is without breath.
So be on guard day and night for death.

2024

BLESSED BE

One better be on guard, for the end of time.
For, we know not the hour of its day's find.
When, we're taken back because we decide.
Not to see the signs as God's prophecy cried.

There's still time to change our wicked ways.
And be on the right side at the end time days.
If only we choose to stay awake and then see.
To have our lamps filled with oil, Blessed Be.

2023

END TIMES

The second, coming of Christ, that precedes.
Will be one of tribulation Christians believe.
He's to face the rise of the antichrist to come.
It will be the fall of this world that has begun.

The final test of humankind is in Eschatology.
It pertains with death, and judgment theology.
For the souls of humanity He will then defend.
And will defeat this nemesis at last in the end.

2023

APOCALYPTIC

I did kneel before my resting place to repose at eventide.
Asleep by entering quiescence, so nightmares can reside.
Wary are latent phantoms, unearthed by their awakening.
Blackguards appear with a message to bestow my shaking.
My eyes twitched, visions become a subliminal disclosure.
For this soul relinquishes the shell of a body as a sojourner.
My future state of eternal blessedness is this concealment.
As, spirits unveil with trumpets blowing, in a revealment.

Lamp-stands of gold appear. One is with a piercing voice.
Holding the key to the nether world, there was not a noise.
The morning star, a blaze of fire as alms upon the one sent.
A book of the living is read, for a trial is coming to repent.
As creatures near the throne are with eyes in front and back.
Imitate a lion, an ox, a face of a man, and an eagle to attack.
They each possess six wings with eyes to foretell a prophecy.
Be heaven's open door by spewing out lukewarm hypocrisy.

2

I'm hindered by a dreadful dream my mind cannot conceive.
Doctrine to the end of time released open, so I may believe.
In a scroll forgotten, the gold light is sealed by seven seals.
The sun, the moon, the stars of night for eternity, is revealed.
For amity rides a luminous white horse with a crown of fire.
As the second seal opens, a red horse cries, a drive for dire.
The third seal displays a black horse, bearing a pair of scales.
A beast calls forth a horse sickly green, a disclosure to a tale.

Its rider is death, granted the power to rob the earth of peace.
Allowing mankind to slaughter each other, hatred is released.
By violent earthquakes, shake foundations, hell is unearthed.
As the sun turns black, the stars at night fall from their birth.
When the moon resembles a sea of blood, the sky disappears.
And mountains and islands, then uprooted, obeying adhered.
Hence four angels uphold the comers of life, a manifestation.
I witness the power given, ravaging the world by annihilation.

3

This domain of destruction has the power to control all winds.
It storms til the seal is placed upon the foreheads without sin.
A seventh seal sends revenge, angels blow with trumpets tell.
For hail and fire mixed with blood will beset the gates of hell.
Water on earth turns a red gore as mountains blaze in flames.
As a radiant star crashes the planet, many people die in shame.
Smoke pours from a cursed comet, releasing hordes of locusts.
And scorpions' sting tortures the unsealed for death has no rest.

Tossed and turned with fright, witnessing a dreadful revelation.
My spirit's in disbelief, the horrendous destruction of creation.
This soul returns to a shell, and a body filled with secrets kept.
An inferno will reign upon the land by the scrolls angles wept.
As the chosen, unknown, will be listed in the book of the living.
I awoke from this apocalyptic nightmare with truth to my being.
For tears will weep as loved ones vanish from man's tribulations.
I gazed in a mirror my forehead unsealed was it my imagination.

2003

LESSNESS

Lesser be the ones in heaven

But greater

Be the ones in hell's crater

2024

PURIFICATION

There is no rest after death for the soul weeps.
Within a place not heaven or hell it's the deep.
Abyss where one will go, for their soul is kept.
To be purified from their sins, so they've wept.

Until their time comes for they will be set free.
They are released, from bondage, in purgatory.
For, they're cleansed and renewed by the spirit.
They're now worthy to behold His endearment.

2024

SO BE IT

There is nothing one can do to change what will come.
One can only look within themselves to alter outcome.
Of their own destiny when the end of the world is here.
Will one be with angels or damned with demons in fear.
It is up to you to make the decision, no one is innocent.
Or guilty of not knowing mankind's judgment, so be it.

2023

INEVITABLE

Inevitably no matter how hard one tries
In the end, you're not getting out alive!

2020

SHEOL

Distress will come to those in conflict.
A punishment of agitation will, inflict.
In a place they will find when they die.
For the abode of the dead they will cry.

It's resting place of departed souls to be.
Never to gather at a table with Him free.
They are tormented with Hades in death.
Within Sheol is a suffering never to rest.

2024

SHILOH

Peace will come to those that believe.
A gift of abundance they will achieve.
In a place they assemble before Judah.
For, "He whose it is," may find a love.

Tranquil be the heart of those He finds.
And gather at a table, with Him to dine.
They are rewarded with everlasting life.
Within Shiloh is its peace of an afterlife.

2024

UTOPIA

Somewhere beyond one's imagination the ether dwells
The place of complete euphoria where there is no hell
Closed eye the one door to this celestial promised land
Its sleep becomes the voyage from reality in each man
For those once there mere return compels one to weep
By a death from this world one enters eternity to keep

2004

UNVEILING

The truth to the afterlife may be hidden.
For the journey to get there is forbidden.
Within secrets that no one's been shown.
Only in death is an unveiling then known.

But two have been chosen to receive this.
Through visions and dreams, is their gift.
By Saint Peter and Paul reveals an image.
As Hellenistic is an apocalypse, message.

2019

TO DIE IS TO LIVE

To die is to live, for that is what it gives.
One enters into the light within the night.
You're without body there, without care.
For the soul lives forever to die is never.

2023

HERE AFTER

Here after we will never die
It's at our death life is to lie
Be within the soul to live on
And to be free a pain is gone
When in heaven just laughter
There is no sorrow here after

2024

TIMELESS

There is no time when dealing with death.
A clock is in the past, one without, breath.
For time never ends it just goes on and on.

From the minute one dies, a demise begun.
It's a journey, in it for the long run, at best.
Eternity ends never, death, forever timeless.

2023

EVER AFTER

There is no dying, there is only, the here after.
When a body dies a soul will have its laughter.
As it lives on forever, and it never sees an end.
Eternity is a soul's home for there it's to begin.
Within the universe as stars that shines on ever.
And ever more, even if the earth dies long after.

2024

ETERNITY

Life in death is forever
It goes on and on and ends never!

2018

INFINITE

How long is forever have you ever wondered.
And sat down to think the days are numbered.
It's beyond your imagination, anything to see.
What can never end, and is always there to be.

Life is so short to what death will be to come.
When we die a new existence will just begun.
And live on forever, without body but a spirit.
For, we are to enter its door to a world infinite.

2024

MOMENTOUS

Look into the future, and there you will find.
The reason for living is by a creator's design.
We are meant for great things, with our birth.
But greatest will be death as one leaves Earth.
For this is a momentous moment to find there.
When we crossover, and breathe heaven's air.

2023

PASSING BY

As I am passing by
I looked upon my life, what I have tried
What I will do, a view upon my life
As I am passing by
For life goes by so quickly, so quickly
With not enough time to touch, taste and see
I looked upon a view of my life
As I am passing by
I looked beyond to my death, without breath
By transformation, to a view beyond my death
As I am passing by
For death comes by so quickly, so quickly
With not enough time to touch, taste and see
I looked beyond to a view of my death
As I am passing by

2004

PASSING AWAY

I know there will be a time I am no longer here.
Even though I know I know not the hour to fear.
For, we all must die, and leave this body to find.
A new home for souls is new conscious of mind.
So I live my life as though it is my last each day.
One does not know the hour when passing away.

2024

DEAD END

That's the way it's always been.
Death begins at life's dead end.
That's the way it will always be.
Death begins and life is set free.

2008

STAY AWAKE

No one knows the hour when death will come
The bridegroom will appear, when life is done
And take, your hand, to be wed, in the afterlife
To be together forever as a couple this new life
Be on guard no one knows when death will take
A soul as a bride so be prepared, and stay awake

2024

DEATH CAN DANCE

Everyone is asked to dance with the reaper
Twirled and whirled into the ground deeper

He takes our hand and leads us in this waltz
To dance the last dance enter death's vault

For soon his partner will be out of breath
Their life is done when dancing with death

So be aware of this reaper's debonair stance
Not fooled by his charm as death can dance

2008

QUIESCENCE

Quiet the mind, and find peace there.
Make not a move but you'll go there.
To a place, life's troubles are set free.
Where, time is erased and nothing be.
For worry will die when one is asleep.
And death a quiescence state for keeps.

2023

EVANESCE
(Heaven Sent)

Man's existence dies flesh fading from sight
Souls are consumed in flames as stars at night
Creation upon the earth forever is in transience
For time in life be measured by its evanescence
Thus, a blink of an eye depicts birth to demise
Mankind is to vanish to an after life of surmise
And our human bodies forgot within a universe
To journey by eternal rest, our spirits disperse
Within God's empyrean is our evangel, destiny
As vaporized stars, a galaxy of endless serenity
A soul is on this planet, moments of evanescent
Unaware death's invitation is being heaven sent

2003

HEAVEN'S WAY

The arrow points straight and narrow.
When death is upon us like a sparrow.
We fly above luminous clouds so high.
To make way to the pearly gate's eye.

That sees goodness of the soul within.
For that is the key to let one's spirit in.
And be with God and his angels I pray.
Death will take my hand heaven's way.

2023

WHERE DO WE GO

Where do we go
When death takes man

Heaven above
Or hell to be damned

Where do we go
When a light calls your name

To that special place
For there love reigns

Where do we go
When the dark stakes its claim

To the fire below
Forever in pain

Where do we go
When death takes man

Heaven above
Or hell to be damned

2011

HEAVEN'S MYSTERY

I don't want to wake up dead
When there's too much ahead
For me now

But death will take my hand
To the promise land
Heaven's vow

Of a celestial place
Where all time is erased
Eternity is somehow

First I must wake up dead
So there's nothing instead
But a plow

2018

NOTHING FOR GRANTED

Take nothing for granted on the highway of life.
One may be riding in luxury or thumbing strife.
Either way the journey's the same where we go.
As we'll meet at the road's end then we'll know.
The baggage we carried doesn't mean anything.
Everything accumulated here, we cannot bring.
So lighten your load, and live life with a smile.
Take nothing for granted to be thankful awhile.

2023

LET THINGS BE

Everything accumulated in the end doesn't matter.
As it only takes up space and will eventually tatter.
Nothing in this world was meant to live on forever.
Even you will be gone your existence will be never.
But that just means the spirit of a soul was sent free.
And in the end it doesn't matter as one let things be.

2023

DEAD SPACE

There are no luggage racks on a hearse
You can't take it with you is the curse
Many have tried to pay with their purse
But in the end has made matters worse
There are no luggage racks on a hearse

Here within we eventually have to face
The coldness and darkness of this place
With no where to go, there is no haste
When one finds they lie in dead space
Here within we eventually have to face

There are no luggage racks on a hearse
You can't take it with you is the curse
Many have tried to pay with their purse
But in the end has made matters worse
There are no luggage racks on a hearse

2008

DEATH WILL COME

There is one thing for certain.
When, life has closed its curtain.
And your breath has gone away.
For the day can no longer stay.

But the night takes your hand.
Then a light will guide His plan.
When, the afterlife is to succumb.
Essence gone, death will come.

2023

REVENANT

Black is the night that has taken me.
Into the bright light, so I cannot see.
To an unknown place another world.
As I float in space I'm being hurled.
Into a cosmic cloud, it's inner peace.
But, I'm not allowed I'll be released.
So, I'll come back to life from death.
And enter once again with my breath.

2018

BRING ME TO LIFE

On my death bed as I breathe my last breath.
I wait for His presence to appear at my death.
It is then my soul will enter into this afterlife.
Dead to this world, but He'll bring me to life.

2024

ONE'S SAFETY BOX

One will feel safe
From this place
When they are placed
Within death's case

2006

CLOSURE

When the coffin closes and one is there alone
The spirit lingers within a body bearing stone
Its luminary light fades to the world beyond
Remembering times by one's memory's fond
This has been home for celestial soul to keep
The door to this universe closes eyes to weep
A tear on the cheek may be mistaken for dew
As a final goodbye from one's journey, anew

2004

RIDDANCE

One's deliverance
From fear's interference
A good riddance

2006

DECLUTTER

You're in the gutter,
When your mind is filled with clutter,
Stop collecting negative thoughts,
By being a hoarder.

Start having positive thoughts,
By being a sorter,
You can discern one from the other,
It's time to be happy so just declutter.

2011

PEACEFULNESS

Within a prayer you may find it there.
A peaceful place where there is no trace.
And worries be gone if one is quiet long.
Within a prayer you may find it there.

2024

HEARTFELT

There are no words to express, the love inside.
My mind tries to comprehend its feeling I hide.
As I take the time to pray, for all that I'm blest.
When, I'm at home or at church as God's guest.
I swallow my pride, and before the Lord I knelt.
To show reverence to Him that is truly heartfelt.

2024

DIVINE DIRECTION

Worry never wins
When prayer begins

2018

PEACE OF MIND

I open my eyes to another world when I sit in silence.
When, my eyes are closed, as I leave behind violence.
I'll travel beyond to a place, where I'm able to be free.
And truly believe there's a loving, higher power in me.
For, there's nothing in our world that radiates this kind.
As I sit and pray with spiritual energy is peace of mind.

2023

A FATHER'S LOVE

It's stronger than the strongest bond
That holds together, never broken gone

Deeper than the deepest, blue sea
That swims aquatic life, living free

Higher than the highest mount
That touches the wondrous sky no doubt

Brighter than the brightest, twinkling star
That shines each night from afar

And wider than the longest arms spread apart
That is how much a father's love is in your heart

2019

BEHIND HER, HE STOOD
(Joseph)

A carpenter by trade, he comes upon the stage.
He's to take her as his wife with also her strife.
Known she could be stoned, leaving her alone.
But, believing she's good, behind her he stood.

A journey, they must go for a census to show.
They're bound to Bethlehem, where he began.
No one, there able is the prophecy of a stable.
He prays from his hood, behind her he stood.

As angels, gave praise and shepherds amazed.
Her blest son is born, as demons are, scorned.
He will be in God's place, but only backstage.
A carpenter by his wood, behind her he stood.

2007

LOVE

Love is a butterfly.

Her tender

wings ache with each

caress of velvet.

Fluttering

to the heavens.

1974

PLUMS AND ROSES

For Mother's Day will always have a special place in my heart.
As I remember memories of my mother so dear from the start.
My sister and I would gather wild flowers growing in the field.
And picking only the reddest clusters Mother Nature did yield.
With our tiny fingers caressing the gift anxious to take it home.
But it was never complete until we picked the ripe fruit grown.
For two little girls hurried home, with smiles and runny noses.
Who, proudly gave a Mother's Day gift of plums and red roses.

2012

MOTHER

Mother another word for love
Who, is sent from above
And is blest by celestial grace
For, she will take God's place
While here on earth, heaven's way
Together again someday
Mother another word for love

Mother another word for hope
So her family may cope
When she has been released
To be with God's eternal peace
For her life will always stay
Within our hearts we pray
Mother another word for hope

2022

LOVE ME MOMMY

I'm here in your womb only a seed
But I have a soul and able to bleed
If I had a voice I surely would cry
I just want to live I don't want to die
All I want is you to hold me and rock me
When all I want is you to love me mommy

I'm here in your womb months have gone by
But I have a heartbeat I don't want to die
I feel the cold instruments pulling me apart
As I try to find shelter by my mother's heart
When all I want is you to hold me and rock me
All I want is you to love me mommy

I'm here in your womb third trimester underway
But I'm not quite ready to be born today
My head is crushed as I am pulled through
The birth canal that would be my birthday too
All I want is you to hold me and rock me
When all I want is you to love me mommy

I'm here in your womb today is the day
But a decision made I'm not a human they say
Instead of my birthday my birth is my death
I'm delivered into this world without my breath
When all I want is you to hold me and rock me
All I want is you to love me mommy

2023

A MOTHER'S PRAYER

From the time a child is born.
And long to when they're grown.
A mother will keep you warm.
Within her heart you'll be known.
For God will hear her prayers.
The many blessings she will say.
I will place them in your care.
So please look after them today.
By, granting me the guidance.
As I protect them in your place.
I pray I'm blest with patience.
And love for them upon my face.

2020

LITTLE PRAYER BOOK

Held in the hands of my mother
She pray every night I remember
To our Father in heaven up above
And read every page with her love

But when an angel flew her away
She still held in her hands to stay
The words of our Father she took
Be forever, her little prayer book

2011

MORNING

Awake to a new beginning of day
Sunrise is the angelic hour to play
Be God's open door His dominion
A shield held as heaven's guardian
For divine spirits appear as silence
Defend man's virtue from violence
A veil conceals the astral invisible
Their task is unknown by principle
Angels enter morning gift of peace
Banish evening's evil devil's seize
From dawn until eyes close at rest
Children of all ages eternally blest

2003

BY MY SIDE

Since the hour of my birth a light is by my side.
My guardian angel is there to help and to guide.
As I journey through life, I try to live, to be one.
I am an example to others as my angel's become.

Since the hour of my death, a light is by my side.
An angel's there for comfort to help and to guide.
For I enter into death's journey, I won't, be alone.
They've been by my side till the end, I've known.

2024

FORGIVE ME

Forgive me for being of childish ways
I was but a child during those days
My world perished in a lone night
Replaced by a surrogate, disguised as fright

Guile angels procure you swiftly away
To never appear destined to stay
Yesterday memories I chose to remember
Death will keep your beauty forever

Forgive me for being so selfish
I was but a child when I made my wish
My deluded memory belie
I did not apprise, goodbye

2003

OUR GUARDIAN ANGEL

Silence sings amid a school's curb
As five children sit huddled, undisturbed
They've gathered together feeling the cold
Their mom has died, they were told
A mother no longer can give them care
When death has taken her away somewhere
But a guardian angel still looks after them
For they are unaware she is holding them

Silence sings within these walls
As five children sit huddled, small
They've gathered together not letting go
Near her casket that carries her so
A mother no longer can give them care
When she's cold as the night lying there
But a guardian angel still looks after them
For they are unaware she is holding them

2019

LIVING MEMORY

Tears of rain

Measure the pain

The death of you

But it does not mean

Not being seen

The loss of you

Forever in our heart

You'll never be apart

From your family who

Keeps your memory alive

And always remember why

We love you

2011

JOANNA
(11-13-69)

It seems it was only a dream
So many years ago
When my father woke me from a dream
And said, there is something you need to know
Your mother is doing fine and our baby was born
But, listen to me closely and he slowly whispered
Your mother is doing fine and our baby was born
But, the Lord will be taking home your new sister
And to this day I will always miss her

2006

WITH WINGS TO GO HOME

An angel flew from my womb
as a butterfly from a cocoon
with wings to go home.
A little one's soul taken and torn
my heart cries a mother's mourn
for this world thou shall not know.

Heaven will give you a name
God has taken away my blame
with wings to go home.
An angel forever blessed
love's blanket has caressed
for this world thou shall not know.

I have no reason to grieve
eternally safe and warm I believe
with wings to go home.
I will hold you in my dreams
you were not in life's scheme
for this world thou shall not know.

An angel flew from my womb
as a butterfly from a cocoon
with wings to go home.
A little one's soul taken and torn
my heart cries a mother's mourn
for this world thou shall not know.

2001

ANGEL EYES

A mother cries when her little one dies.
The sadness it sings is the loss it brings.
And family will try her grief will deny.
For anything good alone she has stood.

A mother ask why when a little one dies.
If only she could sleep her tears do weep.
And so much more is a blanket's warmth.
For a child's heart beat a memory to keep.

A mother will try when her little one dies.
To never forget her child there's no regret.
And believe again in good maybe it could.
Be wings in the sky her child's angel eyes.

2009

SEQUENT

I held your hand being you were so young,
Your miniature fingers disappearing in mine,
I won't let go, a life's walk has begun,
A change lies beside this one moment in time.

For the years come and go, a circlet in time,
Being, it is my hand held, I am not so young,
Your fingers will no longer disappear in mine,
Don't let me go a death's walk has begun.

2005

DANCING IN HEAVEN

When I was very young,
dad would twirl me around.
As I stepped on his shoes,
dancing in our living room.

Now, at dreams' will
dad will twirl me still.
As I hold his hands,
dancing in heaven.

2005

JUST LIKE
Dedicated to Aunt Joan

Nothing compares to the death of a mother.
When the pain is so great, the child suffers.
To leave behind the loss of a mother's love.
For, there's no one to replace the one above.

That is what I thought when our mother dies.
But there was in her place an angel surprise.
And just like our mother her sister was there.
Who, was just like our mother in loving care.

2023

FAMILIES ARE FOREVER

Families are forever
As memories to be treasured
For nothing can be measured
The love from each member
So no matter just remember
Families are forever

2011

REMEMBER SEPTEMBER

There were blue skies

And rain cloud cries

There were trees blowing

And end of summer showing

There were many faces

And hometown places

There were smiles to see

And sadness will be

There were planes in the sky

And love ones to die

That day in September

We must always remember

2012

FORGIVENESS

There is one undeniable truth to heal wounds afflicted.
Bare the venom of sin our fathers' inherited addicted.
Open the hearts of many by extending hands of mercy.
Hoping an out stretched hand seeks others mirthfully.
To look beyond our differences to see we are the same.
You and I the world's problem, and we are all to blame.
Be the solution, the destruction of hatred in willingness.
We are amid angels to look upon man with forgiveness.

2004

FAMILY REUNION

Grandpas and grandmas

Moms and dads

Brothers and sisters

Aunts and uncles

And cousins, too

We dearly miss

Are waiting beyond

For the glorious day

When in death

Every loved one

Will be together again

At the grandest

Family reunion, ever

2011

LIFE WILL BE

Life will be

Let myself free

And fly at will

Worries, be still

Spread my wings

Living will sing

Let myself free

Life will be

2012

SOMEWHERE

Where, the leaves entwine within the limbs of trees
   Different in shape, although the same shape
   Different in color, although the same color

Where, the snowflakes flutter in the winter breeze
   Different in shape, although the same shape
   Different in color, although the same color

Where, the sand becomes beaches caressing the seas
   Different in shape, although the same shape
   Different in color, although the same color

Where, the children born to expectant mothers to be
   Different in shape, although the same shape
   Different in color, although the same color

2005

NO WHERE

No where, I'd rather be than right here.
Not, in the past, or in the future is clear.
For I know exactly this moment in time.
Who I am and what I stand for I am fine.
The world may be chaotic but no not me.
I have peace of Jesus Christ so I am free.

2023

WHAT MAY BE

In the scheme of things tomorrow may be for not.
Who knows what it will bring no one knows a lot.
For one's future is a secret until a new day begins.
And there is no guarantee of outcome until it ends.
Why fret, when there is nothing one can really see.
Because nothing in life for certain to what may be.

2023

HEAVENLY HEIGHTS

Up there somewhere is a sight to behold.
Further than eyes can see or closer home.
Its world is beyond the imagination here.
Or maybe we refuse to believe, it is near.
Our bodies cage the soul until death flies.
And set free to travel to heavenly heights.

2023

ANGEL OF CHAOS

Guardian angel, be near by my bed.
Protect me from evil is here instead.
As safe place for my soul, I do pray.
For I fear an angel of chaos is today.

2023

THE FINAL COUNTDOWN

Its humanity's virtue for nothing else matters.
When this world is in turmoil our lives shatter.
By chaos created within our own selfish deeds.
And now is it too late to repent from evil seeds.

We've nurtured these in the fields of mankind.
For, what do you expect when evil we do find.
The final countdown comes at the end of times.
On a voyage to heaven or hell for one's crimes.

2023

WHAT MATTERS MOST

Look around you and what do you see.
A world of beauty is beyond these seas.
We live together all Mankind we share.
The earth our home no others compare.
We're in this space from coast to coast.
It is love for others what matters most.

Look around you and what do you see.
A world of beauty is beyond these seas.
We're not alone in this universe shared.
When a place beyond doesn't compare.
Heaven is Father, Son and Holy Ghost.
For their love for us what matters most.

2020

HOLY OF HOLIES

Within your heart is a special place.
It is where, Lord Jesus, to embrace.
And make one sacred in God's eyes.

For it is there, we come, and realize.
Our bodies are a temple forever free.
He is in our hearts the holy of holies.

2024

WHAT MATTERS

It's the heart that matters
For everything else tatters
So when looks fade away
The heart will always stay

2012

LOVE MATTERS MOST

Look around you and what do you see.
The people of the world just like me.
And you with many colors and shapes.
We are born with and cannot escape.
No one is better, than the other in line.
For, our destiny is the same in time.
There is no reason, for hatred in those.
When, in reality, love matters most.

2020

THE DEAD

Do not fear the one image of death in your head
For, there is no thing as death when you're dead
No one really dies, but lives within another state
You're without skin and bones entering this gate
But a cosmic realm where the spirit lives instead
And the body is forsaken when living when dead

2023

NEARLY TIME

The time is near when, days will be gone.
And night will take dawn before too long.
For death doesn't ask for permission here.
It comes as it well pleases, when it is near.
So live each day as if it is your last to find.
One will never know when, it is your time.

2024

A QUESTION

How long do I have in this world
A question I often ask
My life has been an artist mural
Will, tomorrow be my last
How, then should my last day be painted
Will, the colors be a brilliant hue
Hoping my life be not tainted
With regrets I did not do

2001

DEAD TIRED

I'll sleep when I'm dead
There's too much a head
To lay in the null

I'll keep then from bed
So my self won't dread
Not living life full

2011

MY LAST BREATH

Will I, savor the flavor, of my last breath.
And remember the memories before death.
Will I, take a deep gasp of air before I die.
And fight to the bitter end, wanting to cry.
Will I, scream at demons waiting at a door.
And pray for angels to rescue me evermore.
Will I, take the hand and walk into the light.
And not look back to its darkness of a night.
Will I, be thankful for the life, before death.
And let go to its demise with my last breath.

2022

MY DEMISE

I lay and ponder and sometimes wonder
On how it will be when I am set free
From this body at rest while family and guests
Come say their goodbyes, I hear their cries
So this is how it will be when I am set free
Then please don't say goodbye at my demise
I'll always be there, in memory that's where
You can gaze at a star so I won't be very far
Looking down from my rest at family and guests

2011

WEAR RED INSTEAD

There are no tears allowed within my funeral's crowd.

I want you to celebrate that day when I'm on my way.

I'll be in a far better place where all suffering is erased.

And tranquil peace is found with the joy of love around.

So please do wear red instead when I'm buried and dead.

2012

AFTERLIFE

When I die, will I, still be alive after my death.
I leave my body, but does my soul have breath.
Will my walk be floating like I have no weight.
Or do you fly with the angels to the pearly gate.

Maybe it is only consciousness that will live on.
There is no need for a body, when you are gone.
One's life source, are stars, lighting up the night.
We return as cosmic energy entering an afterlife.

2023

PROCUL HARUN

Far beyond these things is another universe
It is a vast world, where all minds converse
No need to speak in words but with thought
We'll be connected to each other in this plot

Liken oceans on earth as well in outer space
For, the "Man in the Moon" a forgotten face
When on this planet mankind dies at the end
But, far beyond these things, new life begins

2023

REMEMBER ME

Remember me when I am gone.
With the memories that are fond.

Hold them dear within your heart.
To keep them close as we're apart.

Remember me I will always stay.
With you forever in spirit, I pray.

That one day we will meet again.
And have memories with no end.

2011

LIFE AND DEATH

As the saying goes nothing is certain but taxes and death.
That may be so, but I believe life is certain by our breath.
We live on a journey and by our decisions to reach a goal.
Our purpose in life is helping others, thereby a good soul.
Life and death comes as a set, but at the end, is it just one.
Some to die and die forever, as others will die and live on.

2024

VIA DOLOROSA

There is but one way to eternal life.
It's not always joyful but one of strife.
Just as the "Sorrowful Way" that Jesus walked.
We are destined on the same road to be mocked.
For the "Way of Suffering" is the day.
When, we traveled home the one way.

2024

PRECIOUS WOUNDS

The marks on His hands and feet did bleed.

When nailed on the cross with nails indeed.

To be a sign to humanity of all sins be paid.

By its precious blood with His death obeyed.

2024

THE GOOD BOOK

In God's library there is only one book.
It's so good He needs not to take a look.
Into other literary pages that are written.

As they, are of this world and are driven.
And will corrupt the souls, here on Earth.
A good book protect from evil since birth.

2024

LEVITICAL

The book of Leviticus describes the law
Of a moral perception, the temple's wall
Maybe, it pertains to our bodies on earth
A moral conduct we to adhere with birth
It is our duty to live for good of our soul
And, to enter heaven, for that is our goal

2024

BASIC INSTRUCTIONS BEFORE LEAVING EARTH

There is a manual given to humankind
Endowed by our creator, for us to find
And choose His divine direction in life
There is but one road to leave this strife

It is written, so all may follow its guide
Basic instructions within the bible abide
There is a manual given before our birth
Endowed by our creator on leaving earth

2023

REST IN PEACE

Death is going to sleep for a very long time
How peaceful and restful, this you will find
As your body is weightless, flying in the air
Without any worries to hold you down there
When, the afterlife is a place, of perfect ease
And a death is going to sleep so rest in peace

2024

HOME FREE

Dying is a ticket to the other side.
You know you're there when you've died.
Just like a game baseball, we see.
Death is a homerun and we are home free.

2024

VICTORY AND DEFEAT

Death is a symbol for victory and defeat.

We have conquered death, soon to meet.

One must, surrender, in order, to be free.

For victory is when we enter death to be.

And like the cross, worn by, Joan of Arc.

With new life, independence, we embark.

2024

NEVER ALONE

There is no reason to fear, when we are never alone.
God is always near it's our hearts made out of stone.
We need only to listen and truly hear when He talks.
Like stars in the night glisten He is here as you walk.
Open your eyes to see the dear beauty He has shown.
When He's by your side a blessing we're never alone.

2024

ANGEL FEATHERS

Angels are everywhere and they wish it to be known.
For just like the wings of a bird, they too have flown.
One may think, a white feather that is found, it's not.
It is gift from the heavens from an angel to be sought.
So keep an eye to the ground, for what may be found.
A special present from a pinion for an angel is around.

2024

GIFT OF COINS

What a nice surprise when finding loose change.
And looking down and thinking it is not strange.
To pick up a penny or a dime you'll casually see.
But sometimes in the most uncommon places be.
For angels are there, they do want it to be known.
You are not alone as they will leave a gift shown.
Like a shiny coin you uncover nonchalantly there.
Maybe just coincidence or is it an angel that cares.

2024

SALTY ADVICE

Don't rue the day.
But rule the day!

2006

PHARAOH

It was in the "Great House" he did dwell.
For, by his namesake the bible was to tell.
That the king of Egypt ruled over the land.
When, it was there, he did, make his stand.

He did not allow Jewish slaves, to be free.
As they go with Moses in the desert to be.
It was there Ramesse II gave the order no.
He's known within "Exodus" the Pharaoh.

2024

THE ESSENES

They are the Sons of Light.
And the holy elect, to fight.
It was a mystic Jewish role.
Wrote The Dead Sea Scrolls.
And were found in the caves
In Qumran, Jordan, they say.
Our future will be its defense.
They siege Sons of Darkness.

2024

UNDAUNTED

No need to fear, when you have a friend.
One who'll stick by you to the bitter end.
And have your back, when others do flee.
Not even a disagreement like you and me.
How hard can it be to put aside this pride.
To accept each other the love that's inside.

2024

EXODUS

Throughout the ages, many have died
And travelled beyond to the other side
By a mass migration of souls that left
This earthly place while families wept

All will depart on this journey the end
When death takes your hand guides in
The exodus to the afterlife we are there
Its heavenly palace or hell's nightmare

2024

CRUCIFIED SUICIDE

Wrists, nailed open

Death wish hoping

As blood oozes out

His cries, do shout

This innocent man

Dies in God's plan

Demise by suicide

His flesh, crucified

2005

ABBA vs. ALLAH
(Alien vs. Predator)

Within a world's stage two forces soon will meet.
They come upon the stage their forces set to beat.

To destroy and conquer, this winner will take all.
Their mission is to conquer us the sinner in us all.

For, one we will bow to which name do we call.
Bow in prayer for Jehovah or on knees for Allah.

They come upon the stage their forces set to beat.
Within a world's stage two forces soon will meet.

2009

THE SCREAMING ABDABS

When I picture hell, I think of this.
One's soul is constant fearfulness.
Crying out in agony but is unheard.
It's no relief of suffering, no word.

Of comfort, to end one's ore blight.
To be thrown, in the abyss of night.
And one lives death, always in pain.
Knowing they lost a heaven to gain.

2024

TAKE ME HOME

I'm tired Lord, of this hellish place
Of its wickedness that has replaced
What once stood for good and right
For it seems Satan controls the night
And now the day no longer has light
When, his dominions are in our sight
I'm so tired Lord of this hellish place
Of its, wickedness, that has replaced
Common sense has gone out the door
And truth has no meaning like before
I don't understand, why they implore
To do evil acts, they wish, to explore
I am tired Lord, of this, hellish place
Of its wickedness, that has, replaced
What once stood, for good and right
Not afraid take me home to the light

2024

LOOK UP

Look up, to what, is home.
There we're meant to roam.
Heaven will bring us peace.
Our souls on earth released.
It's energy overflowing cup.
To light up a night look up.

2024

FREE AT LAST

Death will break the chains of life.
There's no more bondage by strife.
And stress replaced, feeling of joy.

When, one enters, heaven, to enjoy.
The afterlife as breath is in the past.
Be alive is not breathing free at last.

2024

TEARS OF JOY

There's no need to cry unless joyful tears.
For, God will take away, all of your fears.
When, death is there and takes your hand.
Together you'll travel to the promise land.
For, God, will take away, all of your fears.
There's no need to cry, unless joyful tears.

2024

COMING HOME

At death's door as you turn the knob
Hearing family and friends as they sob
You're torn between leaving them behind
And entering this new place you will find
But when, you walk through its dome
You're not alone, you're coming home

2024

CERTITUDE

Faith is what you make of it
It is within there's no faking it!

2023

NO LONGER AFRAID

There will be a time when fear is unheard.

When, we pass through the door undisturbed.

And nothing in our past will matter again.

For that day is forgotten a new life will begin.

By our death, we will live with love made.

We are at home now and are no longer afraid.

2024

SAFE AND SOUND

I can close my eyes and truly sleep.
When, I'm on my way into the deep.
And vast unknown, but I will know.
That once I'm there it will be shown.

The sky will open with a new place.
I have left my body there is no trace.
Of worries and fears on earth found.
I am home in heaven safe and sound.

2024

DIMENSIONAL

WHEREVER YOU ARE
THERE YOU WILL BE

2024

HOME FOR THE HOLIDAYS

Imagine celebrating Christmas with Jesus.
It's His birthday with angels to receive us.
And share, in the glorious gift, of His love.
As we sit at heaven's table, there up above.
How wondrous it will be, together that day.
When, we're finally home, for the holidays.

2024

WELCOME HOME

Home at last, breathing is in the past.
You've entered its door, life no more.
But a soul lives on, a journey beyond.
Into a heaven's dome, welcome home.

2024

NO REASON TO BE AFRAID

There is no reason to fear, when death is near.
He will be by your side, when it's time to ride.
On that glorious train when there'll be no pain.
And all worries set free, when a new life to be.
Together with Him, when one's ecstasy begins.
Your soul is saved when no reason to be afraid.

2024

www.ingramcontent.com/pod-product-compliance
Lightning Source LLC
LaVergne TN
LVHW091634070526
838199LV00044B/1061